Dogs Love Waffles

Joyce K Schwartze, author
Chrissy M. McDaniel, author
Monika Marzek, illustrator

Two dogs yearn for some breakfast waffles. Will mom help them out?

Copyright 2025 ©

Maple Leaf Publishing Inc.

Hardback ISBN: 979-8-9904083-0-2

Dogs Love Waffles!

Written by Joyce K. Schwartze and Chrissy McDaniel
Illustrated by Monika Marzec

Mom is awake, it's a beautiful day! The toaster is hot and the dogs stop and gaze, for they hope that waffles are coming their way! Because...

Authors Info

Joyce is a retired educator who has loved books and animals her whole life. She has several cats and dogs, including one lovely long-haired German Shepherd named Lady.

Chrissy is a full-time mother and paramedic. She is a life-time animal rescuer and loves her German shepherds! This book was inspired by Taq who wanted waffles with the kids one morning.

Dogs love waffles!

Dogs have kibble and bones that they chew,
children to wrestle with - tasting Mom's shoes--
But without a treat, these pups will be blue...
Because

Dogs love waffles.

Dogs in the east will pine for falafel
Kibble for breakfast would be a debacle
It's not that those things are terribly awful,
It's just that...

Dogs love waffles!

Dogs have balls and sticks that you throw,
in summer the drips of a melting snow cone.
It's not that these things have got to go,
It's just that...

Dogs love waffles!

Their hopes for a yummy will surely be blest
If not by their master, then maybe a guest?
Someone should realize, it's all for the best

Because...

It's so hard for pups to lie by the door while the smell of sweet waffles waft to the floor.
They hope to taste the sweetness galore
because...

Dogs love waffles!

Stickier, crispier, sweeter, and hotter
The thought of these yummies make their mouths water
They hope that someone will drop one;
they oughter!
Because...

Dogs love waffles!

The extra waffles are left on a plate
Out of their reach, but smelling so great
And the puppers are praying that it's not too late!
Because

Dogs love waffles!

But Mom in her wisdom is aware of the fact,
That dogs love a waffle for a midmorning snack.
So they're called with a whistle -- an unselfish act,
Because...,

Dogs love waffles!

www.ingramcontent.com/pod-product-compliance
Lightning Source LLC
Chambersburg PA
CBRC091601290426
43661CB00024BA/1314